A Poetry Archive

Volume 3
Conversations and Collections
2006 - 2008

Frank Prem

Wild Arancini Press
2024

Publication Details

Title: A Poetry Archive -
          Archive Volume 3: Conversations and Collections 2006 - 2008

ISBN: 978-1-923166-17-2 (p-bk)
ISBN: 978-1-923166-18-9 (e-bk)

Published by Wild Arancini Press
Copyright © 2024 Frank Prem
All rights reserved:

No part of this publication may be reproduced, stored in a retrieval system, or transmitted in any form or by any means, electronic, mechanical, photocopying, recording or otherwise, without prior written permission from the publisher and author.
A catalogue record for this book is available from the National Library of Australia.

Book cover design and formatting by WildAranciniPress.com

Excuse me, I wish to speak . . .

Contents

A Poetry Archive Volume 3

About A Poetry Archive Volume 3 1

2006. 5

2007. 93

2008. 127

A Dialogue of Cuts and Bleeds (2008). 205

Author Information. 231

Other Published Works. 235

What Readers Say. 239

Index of Poems 247

A Poetry Archive Volume 3

About A Poetry Archive
Volume 3

ABOUT A POETRY ARCHIVE VOLUME 3

The *A Poetry Archive* series captures the great majority of poetic work undertaken by Frank Prem and not published in dedicated collections elsewhere.

The current collection (*Volume 3*) marks a change in Prem's approach to writing, and adopts a more direct communication with the reader. A more conversational tone that has become characteristic of his later work.

Volume 3 captures work undertaken from 2006 to 2008, incorporating themes within a number of broader collections or sections, including personal responses to the impact of inexplicable trauma.

These writing years show a developing confidence in Prem as a writer, and a hunger to capture and share the small things he encountered. Each of them a universe, complete.

Language Warning

Please note that there are instances of extreme/offensive language used in a small number of the poems in this collection.

2006

alzheimer's in the twenty-first century

didn't christ say

> *what you do*
> *to the least among you*
> *you might as well be doing that to me . . .*

I always thought
he was supposed to have said
something like that

I thought it might have meant
something real

~

I follow things
that politicians say

I listen
through the newspapers

they all seem such godfearers
and every one of them has *faith*
sometimes they fight about
who's got the best

it seems a strange thing
to me
a kind of phenomenon

~

today I read another hard luck tale -
a follow-on -
from the one about the mad-woman
they put in detention
then forgot about for a few months

they were going to truck her off
to some *other* lucky country

turned out
she was one of ours
all along

oh well
I guess sometimes
shit happens that way

but today I read
there had been another one

this one
they had deported away
four years ago

and nobody's seen her since

christ knows where she is now
or if she might be dead

she was *another* one of ours
who slipped through
a safety net
meant to protect us
from the dirty unwashed

the would-be refugees
who *might* be some kind of terrorists
except that terrorists -
I hear -
arrive most times by aeroplane

~

sometimes
when I cast my eye
over the headlines
I feel despair
wonder why I'm battling the odds
to make my small shred of difference
when it hardly seems that anyone cares
anymore
about what happens to the *least* of us

that is not a measure
of what people we are
it seems
or
of who our parents were
before the alzheimer's of this
terrorising twenty-first century
drew a veil
across our vision of justice
our sense of right

~

I believe tomorrow
I'll stay home from work

it's not
that I don't care any-more
but
I just can't find the heart
to face it

movements

#1

it should not cause surprise
that there are terrors
in the pre-dawn morning
at the coldest of hours
before darkness edges into light

#2

the answer to your question
lies in the paradox
of a driving need
for distance and separation
operating in tandem
with the fear of dying alone

#3

sometimes it seems
that there is a very fine line to walk
between mutual pleasures
and subtle exploitation

#4

there is no real basis
for believing that
the co-location
of a toothbrush in the rack
holds significance beyond
courtesy and convenience

#5

many things are done
in the name of love
these are
however
largely false

it is probably the case that
more importance should attach
to those acts which suggest
endurance

#6

it may not take long
on occasion merely a day or two
other times perhaps weeks
but do not doubt
that it will come
and negotiation will not
be of great assistance

#7

it is useful on occasion
to consider implications
and their consequences
before rushing to assume
a vulnerable position

#8

you may wish to reconsider
based on your own assessment
of the capacity you hold
to cope with misadventure

#9

with the passing of time
there sometimes emerges
a level of equilibrium
from within which it is possible
to see things clearly
and with an acceptable sense
of perspective

dog walk poem

he's a good little fella' isn't he
you've got to love your animals
and look after them
just like they are your children

this one here is called 'stumpy'

'stumpy 2' actually

he's about 8 years old

I had 'stumpy 1' for about twelve years
until he had a stroke and died

my name is joe
and I come from holland
about fifty years ago

I know your neighbours

let me tell you about them . . .

we're still new to the town
but walking *lee-lu* daily
is a form of introduction
to dogs and the people that own them

next door are john and barbara
they supply pieces of biscuit
across the fence when we're at work
and loo-ie is alone

the young fellow a couple of doors up
has downe's syndrome
I don't think he's comfortable with dogs
and loo
is usually still barking her pleasure
when we go past
so he makes himself scarce

at the end of the street
teetoo is a shy and retiring type
who has learned to line up for a cuddle
each morning as we wander past

she actually lives over the road
but she's adopted laurie who lives here

he's in his eighties
and she must have decided
that he needed her company
or that life at home with fighting owners
was unacceptable

whatever
it seems that laurie looks after her now
walks and food
she just wanders back home to sleep
just around the corner
in barker street

enter a crab (for magdalena)

it is disturbing

I didn't think that I . . .

I never thought that she . . .

Idon't suppose
I really ever thought at all

now
I can't stop chasing thoughts around
and around
to nowhere

~

never a yachtsman but I have dreamt
of sailing away
over the waters of the bay

riding at anchor
I can see lights shining
from frankston
to sorrento

it seems a good place to stop
through the dark hours
while I await tomorrow morning

~

it is only new
the words haven't sunk in yet
and

there may not be a lot . . .

it may be *amenable*

perhaps they'll slice it out
with no consequence

but the news is still
so new
she doesn't know what it might mean

fears it could be bad

they'll have to open her up
for sure

and in the darkness
anything might happen

she's been told
she needs to be an optimist
but
she's already practicing the word

  goodbye

silently across her lips

and I don't know what to offer
in return

~

the lights fade a little
the sky lightens

my boat and I rock gentle
on the water

I don't know where we're going . . .

with anchor up we'll ride
anywhere the wind blows
my boat and I

as long as we can dream

of lying still and colour

I used to ride each morning
around the places I where I'd set traps
to collect a handful of scrawny bunnies
on my lucky days

I'd set off to check them
before anyone else had risen

I slipped a foot off the pedal one day
when I was wearing open-toed thongs
tore my toes on bitumen

I turned the bike around
went home
put myself and the damage to bed
I pretended that
if I didn't move
I wouldn't feel any pain

I lay very still until she found me there
around lunchtime

~

ma looks grey on the bed
she's beeping every couple of seconds
has so many tubes sticking out
it looks like they've had to hook up her feet
to get a reading of low blood pressure

she's drifting in and out of consciousness
lying very still
and one eye is weeping

I wipe it with a handkerchief
but it still looks shiny -
puffed up and moist -
she doesn't really know

hasn't noticed

she speaks a half-coherent line
about pain control
not working well before
but
it's fine now

and the surgeon breezed through
a while ago
she can't recall what he told her
but
it must be ok

she thinks that's what he said

~

I found rock crystals on the street
when I was young
odd shapes that drew my attention
with flat sides as sheer as glass

I'd hold their smoky clarity
pointed at the sky
towards the sun
thought I might get a glimpse
of the colours that lay beyond

but
the best I ever managed
was opaque

~

pa and me are sitting quiet
in disparate corners

when we came back from lunch
she was seriously sleeping

we look at each other
from across the room
and know there's little either of us can do

he'll wash out her nighties
and I'll go back to work in another town

he says they should be ok now
the worst was not knowing the result
and now it's more about endurance
and willpower

he says he'll keep some colour
in the garden
that might be important he thinks
when she comes home

george's accommodations

in the loam that is his garden
george is scratching

he has a curled three-prong rake
in his hands
breaking the soil

he has worked this same dirt over
for years
summer
green and lush
vibrant growth
winter
the slow white
of cauliflower

embedded pebbles fleck the black
before he roughs it with his prongs

enough disturbance
to allow the rain
to take a weed
should it show itself

~

george is scratching
in the small square
that is his garden

in the back-yard
beside the hens
and other birds he houses

in the loam
the dark black earth
he is creating another accommodation
for things to grow

only a moment

a requiem for my uncle nick

it only took a moment
you were gone

I was going to send a present
this past christmas
just a poem or two
some songs to get inside your head
to give you comfort
or joy

but time . . .

there never was
enough time

~

we are so few in the world
and sometimes

sometimes
it feels too lonely
when the ones that we hold dear
are far away

but we don't have to be alone
if we love someone

if we free our hearts
to let them know

~

it only took a moment
but I still recall the last time
I saw you

you were walking in my town
arm-in-arm
with your sweet lady

I wrote a snapshot
in a poem
about the way you held her close
and the *love you*
that I heard you say

I wrote it to remember you
and never to forget
that I knew you for a moment
such a short time ago

so that I would not forget

is

at night
when we do a last walk
with the dog
or if I'm outside
for whatever reason -

last week it was looking through
the fine mesh of fly-screen
from inside the tent -

I look up at the sky

mostly I hope for moon-less nights
but even when there is no moon
street lights spoil the view
a little

I watch the arrangement of stars
above my head
the dipper
the southern cross

venus and mars
in changing proximity
to the horizon
or moon

at the home of my parents
it's the ropey shape and nature
of the milky way
that catches my eye

I play the cynic
a lot
and I consider that
a good thing
because it asks questions
demands
that some hard work gets done

does not rely on shallow beliefs
that pass the time for someone
who might waste mine

yes
questions work for me
enquiry is just another form
of curiosity
and makes life interesting

don't you think

it's when I look up
at the eternal familiarity
and slow change
of the night-time sky-scape
that my questions
begin to feel meaningless

what is the point of questioning
something so majestic
something
that just is

random knowledge

on this visit
my eyes are burning

the slow fire
around the edges of the lids
that speaks of weariness
and time spent too long
in front of a glowing screen

these are the lines
that fill a vacuum

when I rang
moments ago
there was no reply
leaving a sense of need
to say something
some anything
even if it's only
on pseudo paper . . .

an image in front of me

pixellation
and no more

I have just read a few lines
from whitman
on war

a casual email
brought a depth of emotion
to my eyes
from a man who had seen fighting
back in 1855

I skimmed it
of course

and in passing wished
for stronger lines to flow
from my pen

to have random emailers
whistling my words through ether
in a hundred years
or more

but the sensation of need
passes quickly
and I know that what is true of me
is that I miss you
beside me

be and is at bondi

breakfast at bondi doesn't start
till eight o'clock

the beach is a great half-moon
that begins
rocky
in the east
all houses-on-promontory
then swells
as it curves
to a broad acreage
of yellow sand
and blue-green-white surf

at this hour
the beach sweepers
are still a-scurry
of yellow lights flashing
as they head westward
toward my latte

perched above
on the promenade
the traffic is wet-suits
and surfboards
string-wear and damp feet
bikini cups and all-weather jackets

mountain bikes
rule the footpath

this seems -
even at this hour -
a place for people to *be* . . .

I'm not sure
if it's where
anybody *is*

knowing not sure

it's easy to tip over
into the *all-knowing* mode

I try to avoid that
but it's a persona I get to wear
a lot

sometimes I don't know
when to switch it off
let things go to find their own levels
their own resolutions

I was looking at the waves
yesterday
beyond the surf
the water looked deep
and flat
and solid

I had this passing thought
that
if a person had to walk on water
that'd be the way to do it
across that flat expanse
of green and bay

maybe self-belief and buoyancy
go together

I'm not really sure

allergy to early rising

I ate fish tonight
I'm not supposed to
but it happens

some little schnapper bite . . .

an anchovy . . .

a smear of something
that once had gills
and fins -

crab maybe
or mollusc -

they're all the same
to me

a peril

I don't even like them
but how should I tell
that a white smear
inside some finger food
is lurking

last time I ate these
they were chicken

anyway
I'm better now
reaction gone

I think I'm telling you
just for sympathy
because the hospital rang -
short of staff again -
so I'm off to work at seven

and I don't have time
in a day already planned
and
the things I meant to do
have just become harder

it's the price I pay
I suppose
for taking a day for myself
in the middle of the week

I should have known
it would turn back
upon itself

but
anyway
I miss you

don't stay away
too long

in the opinion of the duck

kwazy

said the duck

but I know
he's a little that way inclined
and there are sometimes things
that need more than a lisp
and a wagging tail

he's been in a funny mood
and there's no telling what
he might come out with

he twirls his finger
in a loco sign
slowly points it
at me

and I guess it means I'm crazy
but I still think he's out of line
when I
am only reverting
to a true-to-form

any rate
I don't know why I steam myself
when it's only the opinion
of a waggling feather-white tail
webbing and a beak

he's only a talking duck
after all
and it's not compulsory
that I should care

blur-talk

I write birds
down from the trees
some days

other times
I just
crap about

it's funny
don't you think
the ways to be
a writer

if that's what this is
and not mere mind-play

I know I told you
I couldn't really write
anymore
but
I snatched a rhyme out of the air
from something
that wasn't there until
I wrote it down

I guess that means
I'm still hanging around
on the fringes
of something
larger than me

don't worry
I see what I've been doing
and I'll stop it
right now

funny how thoughts run
now that I'm tired
like ink
wet on the page

one into the next
until they're un-
decipherable

that's the way I am now
blurring words
with ideas

I forget
what I was saying

purpose (no purpose) but a memory

we should never have to bury
our children

what is the use
of being
and growing
and living
or . . .

anything

if it's not for the young

what happens when tomorrow disappears
in a puff
of smoke

when the things we knew
so clearly
just yesterday
go

where is the secret
to survival
when a purpose
is not a purpose
but a memory

already
a fade away

I wonder . . .

don't *you* wonder . . .

what was the point
of it all

the journey

then suddenly
a wall of fire
rose
separating the path ahead
from the roadmap
etched inside their minds

one moment
was the amount of time
it took

plans cherished
month on month
gone

and now the path
runs sideways
up
with hills to climb

~

alone
inside
where each one dwells

what thoughts arise

one moment
air is light to breathe
then gravity
like a weight from nowhere

how could they not be tempted
sometimes
to turn away

~

the breath -
when taken -
seeks for strength

resolve lives in each others eyes

a turn towards
the steeper slope

a step taken
side by side

the crisis is gone
and a way revealed

perhaps
this is the journey

past presumption

what a voyage a life is

I am amazed

I listened today to a childless girl
casting judgments
on the bad decisions
made by somebody's parents

how they'd spoilt the child
and made him less
than whole
by never letting him grow

how it was *their* fault

well
it would have to be

wouldn't it . . .

you know me
you know my story

the things that I have been
and feared
what I believed I had become

how helpless I was

it wasn't always that way
when I was young

I thought I knew

I suppose
I have always thought
my instincts must be right

even now
see
how I skirt the issue

approaching fallibility takes
a kind of courage
that only grows
with time

it seemed right
to me
then
that *my* children not be baptised

I had a rationale:

>*when they were older*
>*they could decide for themselves*
>*about religion*

>*they might know then*
>*about belief*

>*they would be better able to . . .*

but that was a lie

I knew
they would never
go that way
if it wasn't taken in at birth

and that sunday
after sunday
it would never take at all

and I knew that

   so what

   who cares

probably nothing

probably no-one

but
as the years went by
and trouble
followed trouble

and grief
grew upon grief

I wondered
if I knew anything at all
and I grew certain
that I did not

maybe
if I'd let them be blessed
in the house
where my forebears worshipped . . .

maybe then
it would have turned out
differently

today
I heard a childless girl
bemoaning
what two people had done
as parents

and I was reminded of a time
when I thought I understood

and believed
that my instincts were a guide
to good answers

I have learned
that answers
are illusion

god only knows

god only
knows

and I
am past presumption

the whistling of my father

my father has begun to whistle
when he breathes

not the wheeze that I grew up with -
from asthma -
that constricted my air
in an audible reminder
of weakness
but a genuine
soft
half note
on each exhalation

it seems a way for him to remind himself
that he is still able
despite the self-imposed struggle
against an emphysema
that prematurely denies vitality

it seems a sound of defiance
but petty
and a harbinger of ultimate defeat
despite a mustering of will
and a deep sense
of matters yet to be put to rights
or otherwise repaired

~

this morning we are atop ladders
he
boring holes in timber
with a battery operated electric drill
that may be struggling from an inexplicable loss
of power
or may simply be responding to weakness

I
gazing out across archer street
to the trees and parkland of the broken river
and the inviting blue
that lies behind it

above it

all around us

I am aware
this may be the last such occasion
for I am too old to fill the demanding role
of child-helper to my father
and he
is on the verge
of his own helplessness
and loss of strength

there is no capacity for pleasure
in this shared task
and continued subordination

~

even in autumn
on a day of superficial brightness
and dark reflection
such as this
the touch of warmth
from a persistent sun
can draw both
a sense of ease
and a dull instinctive defensiveness

but eventually
the drill completes the creation
of a circular thoroughfare
through old timber

and my limited role as a clumsy bolt-tightener
comes briefly into play
before we move on
to the next wooden pillar
my father whistling his air
with each movement

~

when I was truly a child
no goal was more desirable
than to win the respect of this man
so adept at the manly crafts
but that is gone now

rage
is a wonderful teacher
and emulation is doom
without prospect

accommodation
is a way to survive
without total loss of heart

standing here
on top of a ladder
I once again fill a small child's role
no more than a helper to pass the tools
and perform the most basic of tasks

but I am conscious now
that *my* breath
is clean
there is no wheeze when I release air

tomorrow
when I wake in the morning
I will again take up
my manly pursuits
and I will excel at them
as is my habit

there will be a day-
perhaps soon -
when my father's portion
of our shared journey
will be resolved

the child role for me
gone forever

I will not forget
that from the top of the ladder
I could see the broken river
and the blue beyond

or that my wheezing stopped
when my father began to whistle

minimising storm damage

when I first challenged the world
they were afraid

advised me
to keep my head down
to play safe
not to rock the boat
lest I start to ship water

I was never good at taking
other people's advice
have to learn it all
the hard way

but in the end
I do learn

and now
whenever they come by
I try to keep
my head down

I play it safe

don't rock the boat

I aim not to take on board
too much stray water

try
to avoid the need
to bail for too long
after they leave

between words

though the time between
one word

and the next

may seem
forever

look

read

this is your thought

I read you

small life

it's cold outside

sunsets
through the big glass
are a fade away
to silhouette
against a winter sky

unblemished

it hasn't rained much
since . . .

I don't know

but today we did drainage control
just in case
we might get a flood

the land is flat and low
this close to the river

it's seems funny
to me
the way nothing much
seems to happen
and yet . . .

somehow we live our lives
and fill them up
with days and dreams and dramas

and it is enough
some nights -
just looking through the window
at the cold clear light
that's fading to sunset again -

for a little life
that holds the world
in every passing moment

power dream

I've been dreaming lately

a recurrent dream

more akin
perhaps
to a vision

a trance

I am powerful . . .

no

I have *a* power

this power

I am able to see
what needs to be done

a holding of breath
to adjust ozone
before a silent whistle
to collect the pollutants of the air
into a column

above the ocean

above the desert

then submergence
underground

returning the fetid air
to an oil-state
re-buried

my dream of power
is a vision of the earth purified
by *my* action
and the feat involved
is one of concentration
and focus

I have been performing this miracle
nightly
for a season
and
I feel curious

   where from

   where to

   why me

   why

power
has always been a mystery

girl song (in red)

acapella

they're giggling before they start

    knocking down microphones

    shuffling

someone is sounding a note

twice

and
again

the *finding* key

all voices sound

    hmmmm

for the first time
together

all voices sound

    hmmmm hmmm hmm

    ooh ooh ah

they're away

moon-bear dancing

half a moon
is lazy in the sky all day
today

think I'll put it in my pocket
for awhile
safe
out of the reach of harm

come walking with me
I'm holding a secret
can you tell
perhaps from the way
I stand

I step in and out of moonbeams
and yellow rays
as though I've rehearsed for it

practice
with the moon

you wouldn't think
that I
could be so nimble

what about you
I mean
look at you

you dance
with a bear manufacturer
of his very own
and patented
moonlight

let it go . . .

I'll let it go
back up to the sky

the day has become evening

hope lives in the compost

god is in the compost

leanne is turning it
giving air
and making sure there's life
after death
and into the great beyond

into
the next thing
the next place

~

what a mess we're in

everywhere we turn
everything we read
each particle touched
seems on a road to
some kind of desert

a hell made for our times

even the people in our lives
are turning into strangers
growing thinner
narrow

shallow
on the surface of sand
blown in like a whisper
of what tomorrow might bring

and we hold to each other
weep in our hearts
shed tears
for the hurt
and dismay

all of this seems to be a test
somehow

all of it is asking us
to do
or think
or know
beyond confusion

and it seems too hard
seems like
it may never end

why should it be *us*
how potent do you suppose
we really *are*

I know my limitations

but I feel better now
today
we held on to each other
and found a strength in *us*

enough to face the day
today

maybe enough
for tomorrow

standing with you
I can face tomorrow

~

the mound outside
is hidden beneath a blanket
I know things are happening
down there

a mystery of creation
and conversion

it's a growing thing

you give it air
to help it evolve

god lives there
deep in the heart
of the compost

book launch

it's a strange feeling
at once the sense of *welcome home*
while -
in the same air -
acute dislocation

to be asked to read
from my new collection
to an invited audience
is undoubtedly an honour

to stand before the room -
hushed to listen
to my voice -
is a focus for nervous energy

to receive accolades
acknowledging a good rendition
discloses a hint
of the old exaltation

but
the explanations of absence
the justifications for withdrawal
the curiosity of the old crowd
are the excuse to withdraw discretely. . .

to retreat
at the first opportunity

now
there is a strange sense of disturbance
the writer and the orator
reside only
inside my own head

yet
a desire to dazzle
to perform
is a hinted presence
like some last remnant sensation
of bitter-sweetness
in my mouth

strange indeed

brown dirt and fork tines

she takes joy
from the brown earth

forks it over
for the smile it brings
to see the change
that a buried week
can bring

today the grass
and clippings
and assorted things
show a powder -
white -
that wasn't there the last time

and at the bottom
right down below the heat
that rises from the heart
she takes joy

for there is brown dirt
rising on the tines

dirty dreams and dry

and each new day
seems
a terrible wonder

sudden smite
the well is dry

dirt-foul-brown
the stain is a crack
through the heart

pray for water

to cleanse the night

pray for water
for rain

pray

dreams like these
pain my eyes

yellow mellow; desiccation north

on the radio
in the car
when I was driving home
the weatherman was chatting
to ms drive time

   ... and at home we say
   if it's yellow
   let it mellow
   if it's brown
   flush it on down ...

and then they went on
to talk about
using buckets at home
in the shower

especially for the water that runs away
until the hot kicks in

just like we do

~

today the government declared
fifty percent -
maybe more -
of this massive continent
is subject to special circumstances

there'll be drought relief
for another two years

each farmer will be able to buy
five thousand dollars worth
of counselling

have his borrowings subsidised
up to around a half
of a million

and maybe he'll decide
to leave the land
his bowl of dust that used to green
in the spring
but
that'll be up to him

and god
perhaps

or maybe this time
it's the last of it

I heard that
in the heart of drought
four each week
find a brand new use
for bailing twine

on the edge of a ripe crop
of un-reason
and a harvest burden handed down
through generations

they swing
bitter kissed by a hot wind
from the north
that whispers desiccation

~

   some days

he said

   our family can go all day
   with just one flush

then gave
a forecast
for tomorrow

fine again

red-eye north

and this
is the *red-eye* to cairns

strip lighting shows an endless procession
of *no smoking* signs
all the way to the captain

time seems suspended
at this height
but it seems somehow
ungodly
and sleep is not close
to eyes
red and blurred

it's a journey
that will go on
until it ends

tonight
we are the flashing red eye
that you and I usually watch
as it progresses across the stars
from the ground at home

it is *we*
who blink
north
through the night

who **questions from a stranger**

elizabeth shepherd fashions

*zoom advertising and
borzi design*

la-vie photo

I'm in a strange town
far north

a man on a mountain bike rides by
on the footpath

a large guy
covered in tats
going somewhere
purposefully

in a strange town
in the far north
and I find myself wondering

who are the people here
what do they do
why did *borzi design* set up here
sharing a shop-front
with *zoom*

why is zoom on top of borzi

the range of small mountains
surrounding cairns
has lushness
and a depth of wooded green
that we don't see down south

the sky has a clarity that is honest
true and clear

I will know
I suppose
all that I need to know

perhaps it has been enough
to think the questions

ribbon reef #5

out on ribbon reef
the parrot fish
are crunching coral

I can hear them
under the water

they are lines
and dots

colours
and beaks

and they do not care
about me
or you
at all

quite a tern

is it a tern

the tender is taking us back
to the mother ship

we have left the beach
and the coral gardens
behind us
and have set out
at a fair clip

breeze ruffling
bubbles streaking beneath the glass
at the bottom of our boat

there is a luminous clarity
to the blue of the water

a white bird
with a distinct black stripe
on its head
has pursued us

working hard into the breeze
to catch up

for a few elegant wing-flaps
it maintains position
just behind the right shoulder
of the tender

a swerve
as it draws level
then works
towards the bows

finally . . .

it has passed us
swapped to the left side

it zooms away with ease
to reach the mother ship
beating us home
by some distance

the bird seems to fling itself
into the water
before rising again
to circle the tender
then is gone

I said

  gave me quite a turn

you laughed
kindly

it has been a wonderful day

sometimes
they turn out
like that

images

you
with a ship-bought red hibiscus
in your hair

~

no-one
can limbo
lower

~

with the cupola
from the base
of a palm frond in your hand
filling it with seeds
and nuts
washed up on the high-tide line
at coconut beach

~

looking vulnerable
a child's smile and face
framed by your version
of our matching hats

~

your joy
when the second face-mask fit
allowing you to snorkel with success
in the shallows
of the swimming pool
on the good ship
reef endeavour

~

watching
from beneath the water

you
suspended thirty feet above
the ocean floor

serene and unafraid

~

returning your thumbs up
as we checked well-being
through masks
above the damsel fish

~

relieving the solemnity
of revering rain forest
and showing respect to crocodiles
by cavorting
among the yellow hibiscus
lining the resort pool

~

with the cupola
from the base
of a palm frond in your hand
returning seeds and nuts
to the high-tide line
at coconut beach
before we leave

~

I have to write them -
my images of you -
now
while we're still at the resort

tomorrow
it will all seem unreal
just a wonderful dream

u-spot-a-wary

you spotted a cassowary

great big blue-and-red-and-black
oddness
of a bird

with wattles

it was quiet
outside our window
and I saw it too

marveled at it

I don't think I'll ever forget

you spotted
a cassowary

forest sounds

there is no silence here

the ocean roar
is within touching distance
and the forest
surrounds our hut

makes an illusion
like rain on the roof
with every passing puff
of breeze

last night it *did* rain
a peaceful rolling
of near-distance drums

this place sounds
like the cleansing of my soul

it surrounds
and embraces

fills me
complete

circling fitzroy

the brown shape
just off the sand
turned into a turtle

we all saw
a ray
cruising in the channel

the first moray
ignored us
exploring cracks and crevasses
on the water-line
more out of the water
than in it

the second eel
was not happy
to be disturbed

left the district
at speed

two small black-tipped sharks
met
did a circle dance
around each other
then moved on

another swam
straight towards us
looked intent on a beaching

then exited
stage right
leaving us with thoughts
of totem animals
dancing in our heads

an entire school
left the water
leaping into the air
as though choreographed . . .

a ballet

the turtle has kept pace
or possibly
it is another

a distant relation
perhaps

no matter
our circumnavigation
of fitzroy island
is complete

hot heads

the guide said

their brains get too hot

we have traveled up
and down
the daintree river

all along the edge of the mangroves
with their tripods and stumps
and snorkels
rising from the mud

breathing air from roots
dropped from the canopy
to submerge
when the tides are right

these swamps are beautiful
in their ugliness

dangerous
for the unwary

and we have found
the nesting places of females -
who occupy their tract of water
possessively -
and we have seen their shapes -
mostly submerged -
tucked away under the low-hanging
branches and leaves

but here
is a large male
at full stretch on the bank -
lifeless -
for all intents and purposes
on each of our three passes

his mouth
is frozen open
in a cavity and teeth-exposing rictus

he hasn't moved
and the guide says

> *they open their mouths*
> *because their brain*
> *gets too hot*

ochre artist

and you have painted yourself
ochre red

from stone
wetted into paste
applied
by hand

you have become
your own expression
of an art
in progress

harmonious breathing

who would have known

the sound
of a thousand leaves
together

is the reminder
of rain
on the roof

two harmonies
from a single breath

biking accident (slight)

little girl
pushing
on her bike
slipping the front wheel out
to get across the road

I didn't see
what came
I just heard the squealing
that went on
too long

thump

and silence

she was ok
just scraped
a little

shaking hands
and a crooked wheel

a little reassurance
then she walked
or wheeled
to home

and we
a little scraped
and shaken

at *what might have been*
to a child
outside our window
on our road

our crossing

you and I
need to be careful too
because

you never know

no
you just never know

rockets oooh

sky rockets
were the family treat
on cracker night

after dark
and before bed-time
for the smaller children

sky rocket time was solemn
because it involved father
carefully
arranging an empty beer bottle
upright
not wobbling or unstable

the rocket
set atop a thin stick
perhaps a foot long

a little longer
than the distance
from bottle top
to ground

father
with his cigarette lighter
would light the fuse

a fizz of sparkles

and
so sudden
in an intensity of light and sound
a reverse meteor
glowing from ground
up to sky

heads craning to follow
until the explosion

   oooh

   another one
   please dad

it's only a month
he says
just one more month
until it rains a rain
to drive this drought
away

as I'm spilling the water
that pooled overhead -
trapped yesterday
in an awning -

I am hoping
with each drop that splashes to ground
this could be a portent

and in a month

maybe less

it will rain like a flood
to wash us clean

I am hoping for joy
through water

and hope
has lightened my heart

2007

a gasp of life

and my dad has lost his air
finally

he walks around now
not many steps at a time

can't manage the gentle slope
of his yard
from front to back
without a pause

cannot explain himself
to my mother
until breath returns

when I mention the possibility
of compensation
for years working
in asbestos
he waves my thought away

what he wants
is his legs back
his strength

air

cigarettes
and the dust
have led to this choking
ignominy
and an end to good life

what's left is the rattle
of conclusion
in the solid wasteland
of his lungs

learning to kook

a whirring sound
like the wet rub
of stone against stone

a cranking attempt
to turn the motor over
that never proceeds
all the way
to ignition

an undercurrent
swelling to overpower
both stone
and motor

but receding
from the point of outburst . . .

of *no return*

there are three of them
in the branches
of a river red gum

fuzzed
with the remnants
of infancy
fully formed
but immature

a trio of kookaburras
on the cusp
of laughter

more usual operation

just this morning
I noted
the lounge room table

pristine clean

at holiday time
it was wiped down
and looking good
but . . .

so unusual

normally it is a clutter
of craft
and books
pens for writing calligraphy

a vase
with left-over flowers

so *kempt*
it seemed unusual

and now
I look again
you've bought new beading bits
and bobs

there are minute mirrors
and shining things

our totem
black and shining
at centre of the tableau

stuff
spreading everywhere
and all the way
to make me smile
at a return
to usual operations

in this house
we are a studio

occult bloods

it has a
dangerous
sound

cold
like witchery

but it refers mainly
to the *secret*

the *hidden*

it is days now
since I last viewed meat
with lust

for intents and purposes
I have become
vegetarian

(hard to believe
I know)

I have become a connoisseur
of aubergine

an appreciator
of fresh rocket
and baby toms
from the garden

the delicacy of home crafted pizza -
with feta -
is an appreciation

and
it is ok

not so hard
as I thought it might be

a self-imposed discipline

and only for a week
or so

actually
the worst of it
is not about the food at all
the food
is quite delicious

but just fancy . . .

grubbing around
the bottom of the bowl
with a toilet brush
trying to spear one that sank
instead of floated

to scoop a specimen
that some stranger has to pick apart
and examine

well . . .

in truth

I am glad
it is a stranger

vertigo

the stadium
is empty

green playing field
grey banks of moulded plastic seating
in the upright position

at repose between events

looking down
a flight of imagination
evokes a shuddering sensation
of my falling body
at near impact
amongst the tiers below

above
the corrugations of a retractable roof
form an illusion
of rapid

unstoppable

descent

this stadium -
even when empty -
hosts events
that make my heart race

atmospheric brooding

even outside
it is still

two in the morning

the heat
has imposed itself

air
is a commodity
in short supply
and there is a weight
as of water
as of an atmosphere
residing on me

what am I doing
awake at this hour
of brooding

perhaps it is my work
where the lives in my hands
are at a teeter point
with my employees
on the scales

will they stay
will they go

will I decide

perhaps it is as simple
as having fallen asleep in the evening
before the usual hour

that happens sometimes
I know

or maybe it is the ghost
who returned yesterday
demanding new payment
for a debt that I
had long abandoned
but . . .

a debt
that I still carry

a price
that wakes me
at two
in a morning

that broods

basil queen

she is the basil queen
ruler
of the kitchen

wild eyed
the cutting board
resounds rhythmically

she chops

maryland maryland
tonight the chicken Maryland
fills the room
with the subtle touches
of the basil queen
from the oven

o
sa-lad
o basil queen

the hue they left behind

two gum leaves -
autumn sun behind them -
are the soft
red-pink hue
of a galahs' breast

they remain
a colour-reminder
after the birds
have flown

only that

*he can be a prick
you know*

he said sagely
relishing the prospect
of retribution -
delayed
but inevitable -

*yes
I know*

mentally cataloguing

sometimes
it's only the good in him
that makes him
worth saving

one day again

one day
the rain will come
again

water will fall
from the sky
like it did when you were a child
and I . . .

will dance to a damp step
in a rhythm
that plays in my mind
like the pitter
and patter
of raindrops

one day
our footsteps will splash
on the road
when we walk

our coats
will be beaded
and damp

they will shine in the light
cast by streetlamps
under cloud

we will wear collars high
against the cold and the wind
and the rain
will fall from the sky
again

beading

brilliant gossamer lines
gleam against the darkness
of night outside the kitchen glass

truly
it is rain

gentle heart
beating on the roof

random spider-beading
down the window

uncertainty attraction

it's like
a hole in my shoe
just beneath my toe

it's letting in
one drip at a time

enough to drown me

an ocean

heaven help me
on the days I can't swim
good lord
look down and hold me

uncertainty is the devil
in the deep blue sea
and I should keep myself safer

away
from temptation

river lullaby

hush
hush baby
the river's not dry

water's going to flow again
by and by

reach into the reeds
a splash
and a wish
see the blur
of a silver-tail fish

old fishy doesn't like it
when we come around
takes a deep breath of water
dives under the ground

rain rain
from the sky

rain rain
softly
river run high

an o for ted lord

all things pass

I heard ted died
just before a saturday

he ran the poetry
at the pub

made statuary
and stone-ware

at the end of his life
he was loved
by the inner city
and the inner circle

and I guess all things do pass

he wasn't always good
wasn't always noble
or strong

but at the end
he found a place
and someone -
a group of people -
to raise him up
above the ordinary

I wonder
how much more than that
can any man need

eagle above

three clouds rising
like solid smoke

like fog

like

.

.

.

substance

ascending billow

bushfire sky
brown and grey and green
and yellow

blue

you are stars

shining heartbeats
pulses purple and red
from a somewhere

a sometime

some when

eagle of the cosmos
dance with me

veil and haze
I wait invitation
to swirl

over rocky ground

today started with screaming

an intellectually disabled girl
telling me

  fuck you

a phrase she's learned
since she got admitted
to the inpatient unit

the guy in the *hdu*
wanted to see me
wanted to use the phone
to call the federal police

something about
a girl that he didn't know
and hadn't ever met
but
she was at risk

he knew in his heart
she was in danger

a young man craving smokes
that he couldn't have today
made a fist at me
tipping into rage
until he spat with each word
he spoke
before he burst into crying

prison wasn't pleasant
he was used
he said like it was *my* fault

at one time today
there were three of them at me

yelling
screaming
pleading
accusing
bearing down and making gestures
that I should not survive

cathy rang to say
was I *okay* . . .

she was worried I might
over-react
might
do something . . .

hasty

then
I had a session with my boss
about the job
and about him and her and them
and they and me
and
when is it all going to change
and should I stay
or go or . . .

what the fuck

what
am I supposed to do
I wonder

I'm not sure
I'm . . .

looking
for a happy landing

a day as an underwater thing

taking stock

looking around

a strange unfinished place
feels like it might be suffering
sur-
reality

nothing feels quite right
not the way
it ought to be

I am a fish today
swimming like a man
with bulging cheeks
holding on tight to a gulp
of air
and pushing water
with my arms

pushing water
fast as I am able

looking for another breath
and thinking thoughts -
in passing -
about gills
fins
weighing ideas on scales

is a man beneath the water
akin
to a mullet
in the air

little men and women
in shoals

my friends the sardines
herrings
eels and slither things
are trekking off to work again

swimming through doors
open or closed
they don't care
they just go

perhaps
there lies the secret
not at all to do with breathing underwater
not at all to do with things
that feel like they ought to be
somewhere else

perhaps it's all just
no-one knows
but I'm still wondering
and creeping up
towards understanding

maybe *there*
is the great mistake

an exit for the pit-bird

a trill to start
the song

yellow bird
golden cage
brightness taken down
into the darkness
to sing

hope
laughter
sun and the blue
of sky

the green of grass
the clear of day
joy

the lightness of a heart

sometimes
the song slows down
like a tune
forgotten

every now and then

every once
in a while

sometimes it's a struggle
to make a sound
for the dark denies

and sometimes
in that darkness
the sound of the pit-bird
dies

change song

there's a grumbling of thunder
and a down-pouring of rain
an atmosphere of moisture
and water lying underneath my feet
again

change is in the air
I'm gasping it in with every breath
I take

if you stand out in the rain too long
you might drown
or catch a cold
you might find yourself sinking down

but it'll bring us water
it'll green the grass up high
it'll wash away the tensions
that have kept us high and dry
and

listen to the thunder
what a pouring down of rain
I'm reveling in the moisture
of the change
splashing across my feet again

unconcentric sound

a gourd
shaped like a pear
shaped like a
tap tap tap
it is a hollow
that you can shake
and hear the seeds
rattle around inside

it is a gourd
you need to scrub it
down to the mould stains
for a pattern to be revealed
on shiny skin
that you can shake
and hear the rattle
of seeds inside

the gourd
under your hands . . .

you are sawing with a blade
taking a slice away

old flesh is mummified
like cotton or mâché -
look
at the funny shapes
of all the seeds inside -

it is not a gourd

it has turned into a hollow

you've cleaned it out
and chopped the end off

it is a delicate shell
now
that weighs no more
than air
under your arm

the seeds sit in a jar
over on the table

it was a gourd
but you have stretched
the deer skin

stuck it down
and stapled
with a braided band
running around the outside

listen

tom tom tom

it has a rhythm
has a beat
it drums a sound
to fill the room
a not quite concentric
gourd sound
in b flat

emergency services: the light hose-man

in a suit
with brass buttons
and a helmet

tugging the hose
to point at the heat
of darkness

a flick of the switch
and he's holding on hard
directing the flow
playing it onto the heart
of the dark

bathing it
from the reservoir
of brightness

he is the bringer
of light

everywhere a drop falls
new light shines

everything the night hides
stands clear

he is the light hose-man
illuminating shadows

2008

the committee meeting

arrrr-y-arrr

said the door
in a conversational way

*don't let me whack you
from behind*

the table came across
all fluttery
from the flash and shine
of the cutlery

*it's knife
very knife
to see you forks again*

the whispers
of the curtains
left much unsaid . . .

not certain

but the overhead lamp
was bright enough
to bathe us all
in a warm low glow

it is often like this
and sometimes bliss

when the utensils
and the fittings
hold occasional sittings

of the committee
charged with trying hard
to speak in the common language
of a cheese and vegemite sandwich

to utter words
all can understand
because
the squeaks
and the thumps
and the creaks
and the bumps
are only noise
and sound
and . . .

frankly . . .

just too bland

a pastoral shimmer

the hay of summer grass
has been cut
and rolled
into bales ranged
all over paddocks
mown down to stubble

this year
there have been seasons

from growth in the spring
to a harvest
husk-dry brown
and light

broken
only by cockatoos
and galahs wheeling
pink-chested and grey

a flock on hot-wind
out of summer
unfolded to the shimmer-line
on the horizon

cicada heat

a cicada call . . .

I can hear it singing

if I close my eyes
it takes me
to where the day is fire
and I am over-heating

a cicada calls
but
I am too hot to care

the air is sullen -
still -
the sun just glares
and blue is all around

I am absorbing heat
have shucked
my clothes

soon . . .

here comes melt down
while
a cicada calls

my ears are ringing

I have closed my eyes

too hot
to care

heat and sweet

there's a sweetness
in the morning air

dew on the grass
touches soft
between my toes
gentle . . .

to lull

the sky is a canvas
intense
waiting for the day
to begin

and above the horizon
the molten orb
seems smooth
but sharp
at the edges

the rising sun
is up
and ready

to assault my senses
in a contest of wills

who can dish out
the heat

who can take it

I can't win
only hope
and hold out

just hang on
until the sweetness
of the morning
the caress
of the dew
refresh me
again

towards contemplation

it's the time of year
the papers
are full of contemplations

every one
has an item
on what it means

about the year gone by
and the state of man
and the shape of things
to come

but this is shepparton
and the search for meaning
here
is a different kind

across the road
the parkland
is baked to almost barren

it is bare
and dusty
while the road outside is
the *rumble - quiet - rumble*

of traffic forging
through a weary emptiness
while traveling nowhere
in the ache of heat
from high above

where is the meaning here

not in the sound
or the look

not in the feel

that is a pounding
that is a grind
back into dust-rising
eddies

across the road
in the aching park
tomorrow is folding beneath my feet
and staying down

I don't read *shepparton*
in the contemplation pages

and didn't find the dust
articulated

so I wonder if it is me . . .

if my philosophy is wrong
or gone
with the greening pastures
that I recall
in faded promises
of what was *meant* to be

what we would -
surely -
become

still

it is only
contemplation
and perhaps
the job has been done

a moving reflection

*heiy frenki
kako si
how are you*

*is been long time
no*

what news you have

*o
you moving house again
this is so often now
no*

*what
you no happy* u tvoj stan –
in you house

o

you go to drugo selo
*the whole new town
huh*

*this is big shifting
for you*

.
 .
  .
   .

*is funny
sometimes
frenki*

*you home
is not where you living
for put feet on couch
in night
no
but is inside you head
u srcu
in you heart*

*pipples sometimes
they make confusions
for what is zbiljno
i sto je iluzija*

*the real and the illusion
no*

*anyway frenki
you make sure
you always got you home
for you and you lianna
in you heart*

*this is best place
doviđenja
hoo roo*

I see you later

flight of the avi-king

I am a landed creature
I mark a place in dust
risen from my footfalls

from here to there
is the journey

take a small step
then follow

one long pace -
pedestrian -
to another viewpoint
where I can gaze in longing
at the skies

~

but
were I to fly
stretch my arms like feather wings
to catch the air

I could rise on vapors
no-one else could see
up and eddy
round the sky
commanding all below

I would d be the avi-king
were I to fly

~

how far can I travel
using only my feet
to get me there

from this *right here and now*
to *tomorrow*
creeping forward inches
at a time

this is one footstep locomotion
with the viewpoint the same -
the sky is still above
I am here below

~

but
when I fly
stretch out my arms
my wings
to catch the air

and rise on hot-breath vapours
that no one else can see . . .

up
into swirling eddies
round the sky
commanding all below

I am
the avi-king
when I fly

so long the shepherd town

one last verse
from the shepherd town

we are leaving

in another morning
we'll be gone from here

east
the sun is on the rise
the car is all packed
the truck
is on the road

behind us
an empty house
and an empty town
and a feeling
that we don't quite belong

maybe
we never quite
belonged

in the shepherd town
the levees wait
for water to rise
but we
have gotten thirsty
waiting

the sun rise
is in the east

the car is packed

the truck
is on the road

this is the last verse
from the shepherd town

so long

so long

silver breeze

did you notice . . .

there are *hills*
all around us

such a lot of
flatness
left behind

and here we are
all set to start anew
beside the silver creek
and poplars

summer leaves are lush

they twist and turn
in a gentle breeze

silver

green

then silver again

sunday morning
the church sounds its bells -
a peal
to the congregation -
the competition
is not sinners
it is the fire brigade
testing
a siren call

this is a little town
surrounded by hills

leaves
are green and silver
in the breeze

only one

the forgetful rain
neglected to fall

thunder in the air
is a distraction

and the clouds
all billow and bluff
looked moist inside
but passed on by

left just a stray raindrop

only *one* stray raindrop
to float down
to the ground
and reach my open hand

that's all

that is all

little mellow shine

hey
little sun little sun
rise up

there is no rain
today

little sun
lay down some rays

shine
mellow gold
on me

and mine

little sun
shine

a hint of colada

a wisp of hot vapour

rain on the road
is rising steam
like a day
in the tropics

chilled rum and ananas
coconut cream
frap ice through the blender
and dredge out the straw hat
of summer

the season is
lay back
in a hammock

and *piña*
is before dinner time

not today

there's no weather
it's just overcast
and grey

no
not weather
only a touch
of moisture
luffed upon a gentle breeze

no weather today

one little ray of sunshine
doesn't count
that warmth
might have come
from anywhere

and the clouds
crossing the sky are going
somewhere else

they are not weather

there is no weather
today

angel-nimbus

there's a sky
full of silver linings
around the grey

the sun of the west
is highlighting
the brightest spots
before dabbling
in colour

and it seems as though
the light is trying
to burst out
through halos

angel-nimbus
in possession of evening

storm breathing in the bathroom

the dog
is off her food today
and in the bathroom
hiding

there's nothing we can do
to make her feel all right

the atmosphere
clutches close -
like a lover
who doesn't know when to let go -
for a breath of air
that is charged with the light
blinking brilliance around the hills

the thunder has had sport
with my ears
and they pop in a cycle
from left to right
so I have to yawn
to set them back again

electricity is striking too close
and too bright
my place
is the bathroom
where I can hide out
with the dog

we are taking short breaths
too fast
and in synchronicity with each other

yet still the rain
won't fall

beyond the thunder

and the calm that follows after
is shrouded and grey

curled fingers
beckon
as they drift
low
towards the plains
and other places

yesterday
was a growl
a roar
an utterance of pain
that would not pass cleanly
but *now*
is almost gone

now
is just an aftermath
lingering a little long

it is only clouds
moving to the plains
and other places
on the way

not yesterday's sun

how can I blame the sun
it was me
who stood there
while it shone

it was my back
exposed
by no one else

and my mistake -
if you'd call it that -
that failed to take account
of nature
and the time of day
and the burnings
gone before

me
who should have known
should have covered up
been protected

but when I was young
the sun above
was my friend

an hour unguarded
was not a crime
to be paid for with skin
so hot and red

when I was young
the next day
I could do it all over again

not today

my head is aching

my back is sore
reminding me to cover up
before I go
outside

this is *now*
and not a day
when I was small
spent in the sun

storm warning

storm warning

it was clear outside
this morning

storm warning

the air was close
a little cloying

storm warning

it clouded up by coffee
the sky deploying

storm warning

a little drop was atmosphere
falling down

storm warning

the thunder sound is clear
oppression dawning

did you read it on the news:

storm warning

sky watch (I)

I watch
for patterns in the sky

clouds and sun
grey or yellow
or blue
high as a small man's
eyes

the dipper
and the cross . . .

forms
within the emission trail
of god

on a circumnavigation
of the universe
leaving signs
directions

and patterns
in the sky

I watch

summer dance

a zephyr plays
among the standing trees
twists the leaves
to silver

to green

to silver again

the ripple runs
a song
whispered to a prim gathering
of potential flutter
eager to sway and weave
against the blue

waiting for the moment
to dance

reaching to the morning
to dance

hold on to today
and dance

breathe the breeze
that twirls to the fleeting tempo
of summer

kiss the open sky

dance

panic attack

he is filling up

breath by over-rapid breath
squeezes into a space
with no room left
for air

no room
in a waving crop
of terrors
raised on a fertile mental acreage

scarified
then sown

it seems odd
the acute awareness he holds
of the weight on his chest
the tightness

he cannot think clearly
but feels a prickling
at the corners of his eyes
calling him to drift away
to a moment of peace
in oblivion

like a distressed dog
mouth open
panting

hands on hips
in the aftermath
of a long distance run
that has gone
nowhere at all
the journey is internal

he longs for sleep

each breath
is tight

valentino with coffee

it's coffee
on café footpath
in the honey-sun
before the day gets high

take an oversize cup
of valentine's . . .

make it strong
and brown

and make it
good and strong

until there's no point
in just walking

hips will sway
and I might be
the near-rhythmic
zambacueca
all the way
to home

so
cha
hold on to my hand
cha cha

I could start flying

cha cha
cha

faith in don (george) juan

she said

   george told me . . .

four times
in five minutes

like his words
were an authority

she is not alone

there's an old woman
in a double-storey
on victoria road
who swears
by what he says

takes his thoughts
as worthy
to be her own

through all the years
when I was small
the phone might ring

   george
   can you call around . . .

   my hot water's broken

   the gutter's sagging

*the tin is loose
and the roof may fall down
to the ground*

and george attended
the houses
of these women
not then old

widowed
and married
or
spinster singled
they all knew who to call

at tea time . . .

at breakfast . . .

at a moment of need . . .

their man would come

   george told me . . .

she said
and it seemed likely enough
that she might have phoned our house
one day
a long time ago

just wood in a year

writer's group exercise: the fruit of our labour

the old plum
we thought might have died
a season ago
is almost gone

but it has struggled on
to another crop
and there's a big harvest
this year

we've picked ten pounds
of blood plums
a couple of the blue
and have buckets
of yellow-gauge
to dispose of

   take out the stones

   stew them in the pot

   render
   till they're fit to sauce

or

into bottles
then
the fowler's

preserved whole behind glass
to grace a cake
come the winter

and tick off
the list of our friends . . .

for each
a container

no . . .

two containers

in a season of plenty
it is right
to share the fruit
of our labour
and an old tree
that may be just dead wood
in a year

oh wind

it's a mournful wind
across the rooftop

through the awnings
on my windows
outside

   ohhhhh

   ohhhhh

keen-song
touches on this mood
the way I'm feeling

   ohhhhh

how can the wind know

how does a day
decide

what process
for the weather to determine
my state of mind

   ohhhhh

and sing

   ohhhhh

enthusiastic wind
is always near
to give air

to call
ohhhhh

  ohhhhh
  ohhhhh
  ohhhhh

water call

I am the sound
of thunder

driving my car
I close my eyes
see myself

arms rising
and a chant
that I have never sang
before

making vibrations
to the sky
making rain fall

making rain fall

I am thunder
chanting
the rain to fall

singing to water

close my eyes
raise my arms

call water

yellow fading journey

it's a sliver moon
as the day goes down

blue is faded
into yellow west
behind the journeying sun

it is coming up
to night time

up to
stars

and later I'll walk
in the darkness
crane my neck
as I go
to watch the outer edge
of the milky way
and wonder

> *which side up*
> *am I standing*

and

> *does the sky*
> *mean I won't fall*

and

> *where could I go to*

there is a sliver moon
as the sun goes down -
should I happen
to accidentally float
that way

while the blue fades
in a yellow westward journey
behind the sun

modest stars

Inspired by the cookie fortune: a modest star never talks to itself

the dark tonight
seems crowded

pinpoint lights
glimmer across an over-population
of sky

I wonder if it might be true

that they are so close
up there
so constant-bumped
that polite
excuse me's
form static
that fills the spaces

or is it anger and explosion
unexplained absences
swallowed
devoured
into places
that were never known before

are there celestial conversations
the big ones full
of bluff-and-brag

about planetary clusters
and
whose galaxy is best
even though
there is no one to listen
or to hear

what is the sound
of a shout
on stellar scale . . .

how many decibels is that

do they never grow weary
those covert
sparkle-and-wink
jostlers of the sky

do they
ever want to leave

is one of them
the streak of white
that shoots across the far-left corner
of my night

not meaning
to draw attention

just a modest star
that never talks to itself
but waves
a burning fire trail
goodbye

what for?

the house is cold
without you here

to say *empty*
doesn't overstate
the case

I keep listening
for the sound of you . . .

hear nothing
but myself
and the dog

who sits in the corner
curled up on herself
the way dogs do
when they are waiting

for a time
or a person -
a cue or a clue -
and hoping
things
went better today

we are waiting
for you
to come home

fading beyond

we are waiting for the rain
that generally comes
at autumn

with the turning of the leaves
from green and silver
into red
and to brown
before they fall

the litter -
like a carpet that I can hear
when I am walking -
is the dry of sticks
yellow grass
and colours gone
the way of seasons

fled beyond
the equinox we celebrated
in our hearts
a soul-clutched handful
of days ago

and when the cumulus rose high
we felt our pulses quicken
absence of the heat
and sun
in a stretch that lasted hours
was worth a hope
and half a smile

but
that day resolved
like the days before
and already autumn
seems as though
it has passed us by

my feet upon the ground
are dust
and crunch
on leaves
faded beyond their colours
to dry powder
blown like empty promises
on autumn air

really

who am I
but a mark on your page

what is the page
but an arrangement of light
on a computer screen

how do you know I am real

how can you tell
which line will read true
which word is a lie
which meaning I intended

whether I cared

the texture on the screen
is yours
not mine
there is no feel of paper
no pressure from the pen
to indent what I wrote
as I tapped at the keyboard
to send you a word
to say

   hello
   this is me

   really

cinquains

#1: bear

Thick fur.
Its pelt suggests
survival in a cold
that bites and grabs, bitter and bleak.
The bear.

#2: stew

Flavour
from the simmer
bubbles up, spills over.
Close your eyes, send your senses to
the stew.

#3: atmospherics

High cloud
across the sky
in streaks that pale the blue.
Thin the sun, steal away the warm.
Cirrus.

#4: form

Conceit
is a structure,
without waste of either
line or syllable, to display
this verse.

just to tell

I started writing in prose
this morning
when I first saw the busy-ness
of three sparrows
flying across the road
into a tree
where they promptly disappeared

I realised -
almost immediately -
that it was a poem in my mind
not *that* kind of story

on our walk
a red-tailed fire finch
separated from its flock
was bobbling
in the creek bed

we stopped to check the colours
before it bounced into the open mouth
of a run-off drain
and I don't know
why I'm telling you

I think I must be celebrating
the fact
of words that I can see
snippet songs I hear
from out of nothing

just to tell you

the knowledge

she said

*now that I have The Knowledge
I can go at any time
raise up my voice to say
goodbye
and leave*

she said

*now that I know
I can stay
for as long as
awhile
right until it's my time
to choose*

*or I might leave it to god
in his wisdom*

*I know there is nothing
to fear
but the road to the moment
is fraught with uncertainty
and maybe of pain
maybe of madness*

or loss of control

she said

*I'm enjoying these last days
The Knowledge sustains
and I can sail with you
again today*

*I will say goodbye
in the morning*

*for now
it's goodnight*

to leneva

the shadow on the hills
gives a depth
that folds an extra dimension
dark and green

it used to be the purple
of *salvation jane*
that made this the road
to leneva
seem
in between someplace
here
and somewhere *over there*

a farm or two
some cattle
on the folded hills
and purple
mr patterson's curse

that colour's gone
the hills are brown -
dry gold -
and deceptive green
but this is still the road
through leneva
at a point that is somewhere
in between
right *here*
and away *over there*

writers

we are writers
why would we stop

there are things to say
all around us

and every time
is minted new

every day
is shaped in ways
that we have never known before

and this is just what writer's do

if you've got awhile
I can write it down

if you spend some time
I'll pen a mini-version
of the truth

I am a writer
there are things to say

I will mint them
new

stolen moon

I stole the moon tonight

it wasn't doing *harm*
wasn't doing any *special good*
but
when I saw a chance I took it
grasped with both my hands
then tucked it away

the sky
still seems full of stars
and I couldn't really claim
that it is *dark*
just
not so light anymore

not the way it used to be

I can't properly explain
what happened in my head

it was an impulse
a fiendish clever moment
I went mad for a heartbeat
or maybe two

then
when I realised what I'd done
I was already halfway
to home

I'm not sure where to put it
and I don't know what
I ought to do

because tonight
without a warning
I reached out
and took the moon

the weekend (of mr clean)

1.

mr clean takes off
his friday tie and shirt

tie to a hanger
shirt to wash

leather pants and studs -
laid out on the queen-size bed -
are ready for the night

2.

slender cheeky-chaps
and lewd gyrations
become
a dark-cornered
velvet heaven
in the throbbing beat
of *the crimson room*

3.

he wakes up
in a strangers bed
again
takes his head into his hands
and holds a trembled breath
then rises
to find a bathroom

4.

mr clean spends sunday
solitaire

doesn't move much
from the couch
or the play of sport
on the tv
that he hardly notices
at all

5.

his shirt is crispy white
the tie a pattern
of yellow spotted-diamonds
beneath a suit
sharp enough to cut
through any dirty
monday questions

the howl

the static wasn't clear
but I think I heard the howl
of the universe

every star flames

each comet has a tale
of woe

planets
run round and round
while meteors burn
alone
and the clouds of magellan
are moody
while their gases form

we walk with long faces -
eyes cast
towards the ground -
and feel like we're the only ones

only me and only you

but
if you listen hard
into the white . . .

tune your senses
up and out

you will hear the sound
of worlds
and voids

that is the howl
of the universe

that kind

there's a light spot
in the grey

I am watching for the sun
in places it cannot be
so my eyes
get caught
on the naked branches
of deciduous trees
underneath a faint suggestion
of the colour
blue

it is that kind
of day

the hat that won the cup

The matrons wore their fashions long -
   drooped sleeves and button collars –
For it came around just once a year.
   The men bemoaned the dollars.
Gowns in lemon, mauve, or red or black,
   with gloves from the Co-op store,
A lovely grey over cow-yard hands
   in elegant rapport.

Hair in a range of shades of blue,
   all permed and curled by Beryl,
And stocking hose, sleek brown or black,
   with shoes as high as peril.
And each woman wore a dainty treat,
   to sink a poor man's heart,
That a thing so strange and flimsy
   cost the price of high-blown art.

Yes, the smiles of men were hard to find,
   and needed some persuasion
On that annual most auspicious day,
   and local big occasion.
For on the busiest day Beryl'd had
   since the morning of Dysart's wedding,
Each dazzling dame wore a marvelous hat,
   each thatched with invisible threading.

    .   .   .   .   .   .

The milliners of Sydney and from Melbourne
   in the south
Wore wider smiles than you or I
   could fit in any mouth.
One, I heard, sent a champagne *'thanks'*,
   all the way from Paris!
But tongues were set alight that day
   by a bloke from Perth, named Harris,

Who'd hired an empty warehouse
   and for five months worked alone
To stitch the wildest head-attire
   a milliner'd ever sewn.
This Harris did a dainty job, but the hat
   was over-large
And to get it to the railway
   it went down the Swan, by barge.

Then overland by special freight
   to preserve each shapely line
From the red bull-dust and dirty air
   that could mangle a hat design.
By prime-mover then, labeled 'EXTRA-WIDE'
   it was delivered on the day,
And a small crane placed it on the head
   of Mrs Gladys Grand-Chalet

    ·   ·   ·   ·   ·   ·

Gladys was credentialed well
  to don the massive hat,
The wife of the club Chief Steward,
  and bigger than most when she sat!
On manoeuvres through the carnival crowd
  they'd part like Moses' sea,
Then fill the space left in her wake -
  the hostess of cup-day tea.

A delicate job this dowager had, t
  ouching hands and kissing air
While constrained in all her movements
  by the monolith on her hair.
When presenting a prize to Breathing Hard,
  just prior the main event
Convergence of wind and a drunk ex-jock
  struck Gladys, and over she went

Onto ground churned into muck and mud
  much earlier in the day.
It wrecked the best of Beryl,
  and threw the hat into the fray
As the horses vacated the mounting yard
  to enter the starters' stalls.
The cup was next, with *Aley-Oop* the short,
  and *Slipper* too prone to falls.

    .   .   .   .   .   .

Now the hat, while rolling down the hill,
  upset the drinker's tent,
Then, through the roses without a hitch,
  re-arranging as it went.
It would have been well if it sailed along
  not veering left or right –
The crowd would settle with a beer, or gin,
  to calm down from the fright –

But the wind was fly, and the hat tacked about
  at the sound of the starter's gun,
Then the horses were off and racing,
  and the cup was being run.
Before the furlong post was passed
  they were jostling for position,
Too Fit was fast but *A Bit To Drink*
  was showing poor condition.

Bouillabaisse lost a jockey, spread broad
  across the rails,
While the favourite, held in check out wide,
  was champing at their tails.
But, never mind the nags out front,
  the late starter might embarrass,
The form guide could not tell you, but –
  it was *out of Perth, by Harris*

.   .   .   .   .   .

Almost flying, on the outside fence,
   it was too wide to seem a threat,
But the bookies started barracking,
   for it was too late to place a bet!
Around the turn and lying fifth,
   three hundred left to go,
Lashes jockey flung the whip,
   but *Lashes* told him *'No!'*

Then, neck and neck beside the favourite,
   they had bolted in the cup,
The crowd could sense an upset
   for *Aley-Oop* could not keep up.
It's history now that the cup that year
   didn't go to any runner.
No horse came first. A no-result.
   They were beaten by a stunner.

It was argued that poor Gladys
   could have claimed it by default,
But she had left, in disrepair,
   gone off and *'done a bolt'*.
And the Harris hat was seen no more,
   it passed the post and flew.
Just where it went no one can say,
   but this tale,
   I swear,
   is true

pastoral mechanics

I am not a carburetor man. Most things mechanical are outside the realm of my range of possibilities. Not so my father, whose hands sing the songs of solder and braze, creating harmonies in many parts as they caress the metals and screws that leave me cold and hyper-aware of my own ineptitude. And so, the day began with worn mower blades that grew twine wrapped around a shaft and then to water within the motor and the inevitable dismantling of a saturated carburetor.

I can't tell you how predictable such a progression has come to seem to me over the years. Each occasion of mechanical mishap subtly swelling, almost unnoticeably, until the point of sudden status change is reached and we are confronted by major melodrama. The task of minutes becoming the preoccupation of hours.

This time, the surprise problem announced itself with the gush of water - pumped rhythmically by a piston - out through the space more usually occupied by a spark plug. Apparently, the downpour two nights ago found its way inside the air-filter hose and into the motor. I almost smiled at the predictability of the event, but maintained sufficient gravity not to interrupt proceedings.

My father has a workshop at the rear of the house allotment. It nestles, in beyond the backyard alongside the vegetable garden, chook shed and a small orchard of plum and pear trees. The mower has been hoisted onto an outdoor trestle so he can see better to dry all the parts.

While he is carefully contemplating the valve from the carburetor and cleaning the apparatus with an oily rag, two hens have assumed a posture. They are facing each other, almost beak to beak, in a frozen tableau – ready for the artist or photographer.

There are currently seven hens and my mother is telling me that having them all laying at once is a problem because they cannot eat so many eggs. Each hen is known by the colour of it's eggs. The black one lays white eggs with a blue-green hue, that brown lays speckles. The white, of course, lays white eggs.

The first reconstruction of the mower has ended precipitously with a flood of fuel. The carburetor valve hasn't gone in properly. Father snaps a vicious short curse aimed squarely at the foul mechanism and commences to pull it apart again.

As though coordinated, three of the hens have started scratching. Two are working in tandem, half hidden in an excavation that has taken considerable effort over a period of time.

A brown one beside me lets fly with a near-liquid expression of good will before clawing the earth backward. A big scratch, followed by close examination with a beady eye, before a follow-up scratch.

The earth is being moved, three toes at a time.

I now hold the mower tilted to an angle that allows access to its nether regions. It appears the base plate has been put back loose. No problem, do it again. This time clean all the parts properly.

The way my father can logically diagnose the nature of each mechanical problem and then the procedure necessary to rectify it seems remarkable to me and my role of holding objects in place and passing tools as required no longer troubles me as it did in younger days. Back then I felt it was my task to exceed him in all areas and activities. Being aware of the flow of his processes and filling a small role as occasion merits has become sufficient.

The dog has now joined the hens. They are relatively new to each other but move easily together – sniffing in this corner, scratching in that.

A quiet *c-a-a-a-w, c-a-a-a-w* makes for a gentle background to the afternoon until the sound of the chook-yard gate opening on the other side of the workshop sets all seven hens running in a frenzied unison of expectation that some new green-feed will have been deposited in the yard. A few moments later a more stately return to previous pursuits has begun and the pleasant softness of the day is reinstituted

At last, the mower is assembled and roaring with good health. Hens and dog, startled, have found more distant areas of the yard to interest them, while my father and I are nodding knowingly at each other about the vagaries of machine engineering and how you can never tell where the first thing that you touch might lead you.

Silence returns and the blue smoke fades. The day has had unexpected turns, and been unexpectedly satisfying. It seems mower maintenance can hold meditative rewards, even for the non-mechanical when the afternoon is lazy, the hens *c-a-a-a-w* and the dog has an interesting notion of a place to explore, while my father and I are each doing the things we do best.

this years harvest

Resistance is useless. The chestnuts are over-ripe and have been falling for two weeks now. If any are to be picked, today is the day.

This is an unusual year and where, at other times, my aunt and uncle might gather and process over a tonne of nuts between them, the season has been forfeited because of my uncle's lingering illness and a forced focus on life above commerce. Today we've assembled as a small family group to collect a token amount, to register the experience and also to declare that the crop was not an entire loss.

At the sheds, before we are turned loose to wander through the orchard with buckets in hand, my aunt checks our protective equipment and finds it deficient – ordinary gardening gloves are out, we need rubber gloves to have any hope of keeping out the tough prickles on the nut casings. Then we are off, beneath the trees.

Shade is thick beneath these twenty-year old trees, each striving to achieve majestic status but in practice a wide-ranging lot varying from a tall elegance to stunted disappointment and the occasional abject failure in the form of a stump and open space between the adjoining canopies. These trees have many years to go before maturity.

The ground is littered with fallen shells that promise pain for the unwary, each a bristling protection for a trove of brown treasure hidden within. The first nuts I collect are in a dry brown casing that opens with a wrench to one side and holds three chestnuts. There is a polished warmth in the rich brown of this fruit and a momentary fascination to examine them in the clear autumn sunlight, like a youth finding a first crystal on the path. The pickings, here, under the first tree are slim, however. Too few nuts yielded for the effort and pain. Another tree may prove better.

My uncle is walking around the shedding of his little farmlet as we work. He bought the ten acres two decades ago and planted the trees as seedlings that he had grown from the nut, then hand-watered until they were established. He keeps hens here, grows vegetables and fruit. His visits to oversee these activities are a daily pleasure.

This last twelve months has seen change, though. The creek that supplies his dam has dried up for the first time in living memory and he himself has had an illness that has kept him away for weeks leading up to harvest time, and so the routines of past years have been up-ended. The crop will be left to lie un-gathered while he walks the perimeters to re-establish contact with the things in his life that he values.

I have found a tree with large, mostly green casings that come apart a little easier in my hands and yield swollen, heavy nuts. The prickling cost of collecting is a constant, sharp needling into my fingers and through my trousers where I have kneeled or sat to facilitate the picking.

My aunt glances into the depths of my unfilled bucket and laughs a little before commenting that she routinely gathers two buckets of nuts to my uncles one. She is a pressure cooker of activity, always on the go and looking for the next thing that needs doing. These last weeks with my uncle in hospital in Melbourne, four hours away, have been even more stressful because she has not been able to stay with him. Twice-weekly visits have only added to her worry and she has been almost frantic in her efforts to keep occupied. My awareness of how difficult this recent time has been for her is heightened by the transparent relief that shows in her movements and the pleasure she is taking from today.

Each casing I open and empty is thrown behind me, out of the perimeter of the canopy of the tree. If this were a serious harvest, it would be important to have the area clear so that the each new fall of nuts on following days would not be confused with the already emptied husks.

Glancing across I can see others using a variety of techniques to get at the nuts. Some are bending from the knees to get down to ground level, some are standing on the casings with their feet and scuffing them to break in to the nuts without getting pricked in the process.

Each picker finds their own rhythm.

Sitting down beneath the tree I think I have done enough. My bucket holds more chestnuts than I'll eat in a decade of seasons and the experience of picking them will sustain me for even longer. My aunt advises me to take what I have picked home and then to empty the bucket on a table. She says to sort out the very big ones - to keep - and to compost the rest. In other years they would use a sorting machine to separate out the various sizes before transport to market, but there is no point in struggling with undersized nuts when there is so much unused crop.

Next years harvest may be different.

everlasting

The everlasting daisy has changed its mind. Over a number of days it had begun to open paper-like petals, purple tipped with white hearts, but an early snow has blanketed the alps and allowed the escape of a brittle layer of frost which now covers the newly planted front garden. The daisy has reconsidered available options and chosen to close up until more favorable omens present themselves.

This embryonic garden has become a symbolic treasure from the moment of your first arguments with the landlord that the application of poison to control the rampant - unapproved - plant-life was both unnecessary and nasty. That the two of us would undertake a comprehensive weed-removal program, good results guaranteed.

For weeks you led us on a hands and knees crusade to painstakingly uproot pondweed and assorted green *bad guys*, with the landlord coaching from the sidelines: *"don't put those into the compost, you'll never get rid of them. Throw them in the rubbish bin . . ."* but the time passed quickly. A session in the morning before the sun grew too hot. Another in the evening when it passed behind the hills on its way down.

Then, a final session of dust as we spread

eucalypt mulch, and experienced the resurrection from a*bandoned wasteland* to *garden in waiting.* We couldn't stop smiling at each other whenever we glanced through the window, or stepped out the door. A sense of arrival through having made our own indelible mark on this dirt.

This morning, you have been transplanting *agi*'s from alongside the neighbours fence to form a green border between us and the road. They are lush and moist. Survivors in all kinds of weather and treatment. A little like you and me.

A Dialogue of Cuts and Bleeds (2008)

atmospheric brooding

even outside
it is still

two in the morning
the heat
has imposed itself

air
is a commodity
in short supply
and there is a weight
as of water
as of
an atmosphere
residing on me

what am I doing
awake at this hour
of brooding

perhaps it is my work
where the lives in my hands
are at a teeter point with staff
on my scales

will they stay
will they go

will *I* decide

perhaps it is as simple
as falling asleep in the evening
before the usual hour

that happens
sometimes
I know

or maybe
it is the ghost
who returned yesterday
demanding new payment
for a debt I had abandoned

a debt
that I carry

with a price
that wakes me at two o'clock
on a morning
that broods

contemplation of the unthinkable

what do you do
when you are told
your child is dying

actually
it isn't even news
really

he has been living
with his own pending death
for fourteen years now

but still
it hits you in the guts

clenching

unclenching

the latest brain scan
sort of makes it worse

his brain is shrinking
so he will actually dement
before he dies

one of the few saving graces
of the ordeal
has been that his personality
was retained
and -
boy and man -
he's been a lovely bloke

a real pleasure

to think of his poor
oxygen starved brain
giving up before the rest of him
is a hard ask

a terrible hard ask

with each contemplation
I come closer to understanding
how some decisions get made
and some actions
taken

then

I knew it then
I know it now

the efforts that I made

> *turning myself
> inside and out*
>
> *lying wakeful
> in the middle of
> long
> nights*
>
> *berating myself*
>
> *railing against injustice*
>
> *despairing sins
> of thought
> and deed*

nothing that I did
was enough

nothing helped

but god alone knew
it was all
that I could

identifying the bastard

melas

c---

I have lived with your name
in my head
for too long

bastard

killer

around blood

blood is the viscous beast

I watch it

my veins . . .

all this time
it has flowed

have you ever tried to measure
a circle

you end up
going around
and around

blood
is the circle
and even after time

after
a long long time

I go around

in other words

> *mitochondrial*
> *myopathy*
> *encephalopathy*
> *lactic acidosis and stroke*
> *(MELAS)*
> *is a progressive neurodegenerative disorder*

where from

> black beast and burden

where from

a blue morning
a golden afternoon

a dark night

> *approximately 80% of patients*
> *with the clinical characteristics*
> *of MELAS*
> *have a heteroplasmic A-to-G point mutation*
> *in the dihydrouridine loop*
> *of the transfer RNA (tRNA)Leu (UUR) gene*
> *at base pair (bp) 3243 (ie, 3243 A->G*
> *mutation)*

> *however*
> *other mitochondrial DNA (mtDNA) mutations*
> *are observed*

including the 3244 G->A
3258 T->C, 3271 T->C
and 3291 T->C
in the mitochondrial tRNALeu(UUR) gene

I don't understand you

enigma

> *the progressive disorder*
> *has a high morbidity and mortality*

> *the encephalomyopathy*
> *associated with strokelike episodes*
> *followed by hemiplegia*
> *and hemianopia*

> *is severe*

your language
is an assault you hide behind
to steal sound
take away sight
remove the vestige
of balance

you stole slowly
you thief
the mind of the flesh of me

took away the last
of innocence
and faith

other abnormalities that may be observed
are ventricular dilatation
cortical atrophy
and basal ganglia calcification

oh oh oh

oh

I can hardly breathe

when I think of you
rage
such pointless empty *rage*

what have you done
to my boy
what need had you
for such a life

oh oh oh
oh

MELAS
displays considerable variability
in presentation
however
patients in general
tend to have
a poor prognosis
and outcome

such a short time
to fill
so long spent
waiting
for the next blow

> *the encephalomyopathy*
> *tends to be severe*
> *and progressive to dementia*

ah
he's still so young

this is not fair

> *the patient with MELAS*
> *may end up in a state*
> *of cachexia*

waste
waste
such a wretched waste
of a life

> *currently*
> *no therapies*
> *have proven efficacy*

which way
lie the pointers

which words
should I use

how
what

nothing explains

nothing resolves

despair
is a progressive disorder

a few edgy words

I seem on the edge
of tears
just lately

fierce and almost angry
in pursuit of my tasks
and confronting distractions
and irrelevancies
and then
in a heartbeat
on the edge

today
just a few words
nearly brought me undone

I felt the need to explain
that some of my irritation
was from a different cause

my son has lost a lot more
of his cognitive abilities
and he's now on the verge
of dementia

when he tips over
the rest of the way
he will probably die

quite quickly I think

I noticed the catch in my throat
immediately
and cut it all short

   well

   see you

   have a good weekend

   bye

it's been a hard week
and I find myself
on edge

with just a few words

travel options

he said he prefers to go
by train

it is better
when there's room to move
and buses are so cramped up

and it is better
if there is no need to change
modes of travel
at seymour

it is easy to get confused
easy to get lost
hard to comprehend just who
to ask
when he finds himself
in trouble

I guess all of us
get into trouble

every day is a minefield
of places not to make false steps

and I've got you
to ask
you've got me

for us
that's just enough
but even alone
we would suffice somehow

our world

option b
is a train that doesn't stop
in seymour

it passes through that town
then out of the hills
alongside open channels

until it gets to here
where we will wait
to meet him safely home

before evening

he is a little like a house
whose lights
are winking out
one

by

one

a silhouette
fading to black
as darkness steals in
too soon

reasons

try as I might
to banish them

try
from the heart
to turn away

not to feel

or know
as I do
that there's nothing left
that I should do

I've attempted it all
and done it before
once or twice
then
maybe more

it all remains

and I remain
not
unaffected

if it were a song
then
moody blue

a tune to be hummed
down hearted

A DIALOGUE OF CUTS AND BLEEDS (2008)

feeling raw

but it isn't a song
it's not really a feeling

but the sound of a voice
from a long time ago

glimpse of a world
left behind

the a taste of a bile
that burned my throat

reminder
of who I was
and what I did
and all those
melancholy reasons

relativity and retreat

today
he is here
on a so-rare visit

a little deterioration
slippage around the margins
but not so bad

not really

I spend my time pondering
relationship

he is in the lounge
watching a midday movie
at my suggestion

I am in the study
making a thought
likewise
at my own whim

according with instructions

so the years go by
and I
receive instructions in the mail
about the way
to conduct a weekend

what to watch
and how to play
and a lecture about the nature
of a son I helped to raise
back then

but this is now
and I'm away
on the outer fringes
of a fatherhood
that has no shape
no form
no place
no reason at all
except
in other minds

and I need to read the mail
a second time
to find a place
between the lines
where I can do a weekend
as required
in accordance with instructions

prayer for the lost

my mother prays for the resurrection
of her child's children
from the ravages
of disease
descended like a scourge unanticipated
and a life spent . . .

not wisely

foolish of love
unwise
of belonging

she wishes to embrace
the prodigal
but all she has is me
inadequate and flawed

I can't tell her clearly
that the children we both weep for
are lost for me
dead and gone
a long while
though I haven't buried
either of them yet

they keep walking through soft places
in our hearts

in my hands I carry flails
with which to blood
my metaphoric back
for a failure of normality. . .

an inability to rise
before challenge

I could not stand
I could not fight

and I pray
just like my mother does
I pray
for an end to masquerades
of life

I pray
to be allowed
to put my sons to rest
to bury
what I lost
a long time ago

Author Information

About the Author

Frank Prem has been a storytelling poet since his teenage years. He has been a psychiatric nurse through all of his professional career, which now exceeds forty years.

He has been published in magazines, online zines, and anthologies in Australia, and in a number of other countries, and has both performed and recorded his work as spoken word.

He lives with his wife in the beautiful township of Beechworth in North East Victoria, Australia.

Connect with Frank

As the author, I hope you enjoyed this volume of poetry collection. I think that mine is a unique style of writing that can appeal well beyond a 'pure poetry' readership.

If you enjoyed it, please feel invited to pop over to my author page www.FrankPrem.com, and subscribe to receive my occasional Newsletter.

From time to time I'll let you know what is happening with myself and my writing, as well as keeping you informed of any giveaways I may be planning.

You can also find me on Facebook, Twitter, Instagram and YouTube.

Other Published Works

Free Verse Poetry

Small Town Kid (2018)
Devil In The Wind (2019)
The New Asylum (2019)
Herja, Devastation - With Cage Dunn (2019)
Walk Away Silver Heart (2020)
A Kiss for the Worthy (2020)
Rescue and Redemption (2020)
Pebbles to Poems (2020)
The Garden Black (2022)
A Specialist at The Recycled Heart (2022)
Ida: Searching for The Jazz Baby (2023)
From Volyn to Kherson (2023)
Alive Is What You Feel (2023)
White Whale (2024)
Pilgrim Volume 1 (2024)

Picture Poetry/Spoken Image

Voices (In The Trash) (2020)
The Beechworth Bakery Bears (2021)
Sheep On The Somme (2021)
Waiting For Frank-Bear (2021)
A Lake Sambell Walk (2021)
A Few Places Near Home (2023)

What Readers Say

Small Town Kid

A modern-day minstrel
Small-Town Kid is a wonderful collection
—S. T. (Australia)
A poet's walk through his childhood in a small Australian town.
—J. L. (USA)

Devil In The Wind

Instantly grips you by the throat in his step-by-step story of survival.
Bravo!
—K. K. (USA)
Outstanding!
—B. T. (Australia)

The New Asylum

> Words can't do justice to the emotional journey I travelled in (reading this collection).
> __C. D. (Australia)
> If I had to pick one book over the past year that has truly resonated with me, this would be it.
> __K. B. (USA)

Walk Away Silver Heart

> Has an extraordinary way with words and his poems invoke great passion and emotion in the reader.
> —R C (United States)
> As Memorable as My Favourite Music
> —M D (United States)

A Kiss For The Worthy

A Celebration of Life Written in Thoughtful Bursts of Poetic Expression
—C M C (United States)

With every verse, I found myself reflecting about myself, my life, and the world.
—K

Rescue and Redemption

The passion of love in its many forms explored by one for another.
—J L (United States)

I've enjoyed every word, every breath. Every moment within the life of these stories.
—C D (Australia)

Sheep On The Somme

> *Museums and archivists take note--sell this in your gift shops, preserve it in your archives. Professors, teachers--share with your students.*
> *—A R C (United States)*
>
> *(This) book is a beautiful and graphic tribute to all those brave men and women who gave their lives for their countries between 1914 and 1918.*
> *—R C (South Africa)*

Ida: Searching for The Jazz Baby

> *I found myself deeply moved by the presentation of Ida's elusive, illusionary life.*
> *—E G (United States)*
>
> *He gives her a depth and vulnerability that the press didn't.*
> *— A C (United Kingdom*

The Garden Black

Prem creates verse that illuminates our world, its experiences and history.
—S C (United Kingdom)

Prem's poetry reminds that life is fragile and fleeting ... both harsh and beautiful.
—D G K (United States)

Herja, Devastation

Simply written, powerfully felt.
__C. (Australia)

As a combination of poetry, prose, and wonderfully ominous illustrations, I found Herja, Devastation refreshingly original. Highly recommended!
—G. B. (Australia)

Bravo! Outstanding!
—B. T. (Australia)

Index of Poems

INDEX OF POEMS

A

according with instructions 227
a day as an underwater thing 119
a few edgy words 219
a gasp of life 95
a hint of colada 148
allergy to early rising 33
alzheimer's in the twenty-first century 7
a moving reflection 138
an exit for the pit-bird 121
angel-nimbus 150
an o for ted lord 113
a pastoral shimmer 131
around blood 213
atmospheric brooding 103, 207

B

basil queen 105
beading 110
be and is at bondi 30
before evening 223
between words 53
beyond the thunder 153
biking accident (slight) 88
blur-talk 37
book launch 64
brown dirt and fork tines 66

C

change song 123
cicada heat 132
cinquains 177
circling fitzroy 82
contemplation of the unthinkable 209

D

dirty dreams and dry 67
dog walk poem 14

E

eagle above 114
emergency services: the light hose-man 126
enter a crab (for magdalena) 16
everlasting 203

F

fading beyond 174
faith in don (george) juan 162
flight of the avi-king 140
forest sounds 81

G

george's accommodations 22
girl song (in red) 58

H

harmonious breathing 87
heat and sweet 133
hope lives in the compost 61
hot heads 84

I

identifying the bastard 212
images 77
in other words 214
in the opinion of the duck 35
is 26

J

just to tell 178
just wood in a year 164

K

knowing not sure 32

L

learning to kook 97
little mellow shine 147

M

minimising storm damage 52
modest stars 171
moon-bear dancing 59
more usual operation 98
movements 11

N

not today 149
not yesterday's sun 154

O

occult bloods 100
ochre artist 86
of lying still and colour 19
oh wind 166
one day again 108
only a moment 24
only one 146
only that 107
over rocky ground 116

P

panic attack 159
pastoral mechanics 195
past presumption 43
power dream 56
prayer for the lost 228
purpose (no purpose) but a memory 39

Q

quite a tern 75

R

random knowledge 28
really 176
reasons 224
red-eye north 71
relativity and retreat 226
ribbon reef #5 74
river lullaby 112
rockets oooh 90

S

silver breeze 144
sky watch (I) 157
small life 54
so long the shepherd town 142
stolen moon 183
storm breathing in the bathroom 151
storm warning 156
summer dance 158

T

that kind 189
the committee meeting 129
the hat that won the cup 190
the howl 187
the hue they left behind 106
the journey 41
the knowledge 179
then 211
the weekend (of mr clean) 185
the whistling of my father 47
this years harvest 199
to leneva 181
towards contemplation 135
travel options 221

U

uncertainty attraction 111

unconcentric sound 124
u-spot-a-wary 80

V

valentino with coffee 161
vertigo 102

W

water call 168
what for? 173
who questions from a stranger 72
writers 182

Y

yellow fading journey 169
yellow mellow; desiccation north 68

www.FrankPrem.com

www.ingramcontent.com/pod-product-compliance
Lightning Source LLC
Chambersburg PA
CBHW072109110526
44590CB00018B/3375